"Some places have already quit lotteries," Mrs. Adams said.

"Nothing but trouble in *that*," Old Man Warner said stoutly. "Pack of young fools."

CREATIVE SHORT STORIES

THE LOTTERY

SHIRLEY JACKSON

CREATIVE EDUCATION

The morning of June 27th was clear and sunny, with the fresh warmth of a full-summer day; the flowers were blossoming profusely and the grass was richly green. The people of the village began to gather in the square, between the post office and the bank, around ten o'clock; in some towns there were so many people that the lottery took two days and had to be started on June 26th, but in this village, where there were only about three hundred people, the whole lottery took less than two hours, so it could begin at ten o'clock in the morning and still be through in time to allow the villagers to get home for noon dinner.

The children assembled first, of course. School was recently over for the summer, and the feeling of liberty sat uneasily on most of them; they tended to gather together quietly for a while before they broke into boisterous play. And their talk was still of the classroom and the teacher, of books and reprimands. Bobby Martin had already stuffed his pockets full of stones, and the other boys soon followed his example, selecting the smoothest and roundest stones; Bobby and Harry Jones and Dickie Delacroix—the villagers pronounced this name "Dellacroy"—eventually made a great pile of stones in one corner of the square and guarded it against the raids of the other boys. The girls stood aside, talking among themselves, looking over their shoulders at the boys, and the very small children rolled in the dust or clung to the hands of their older brothers or sisters.

Soon the men began to gather, surveying their own children, speaking of planting and rain, tractors and taxes. They stood together, away from the pile of stones in the corner, and their jokes were quiet and they smiled rather than laughed. The women, wearing faded housedresses and sweaters, came shortly after their menfolk. They greeted one another and exchanged bits of gossip as they went to join their husbands. Soon the women, standing by their husbands, began to call to their children, and the children came reluctantly, having to be called four or five times. Bobby Martin ducked under his mother's grasping hand and ran, laughing, back to the pile of stones. His father spoke up sharply, and Bobby came quickly and took his place between his father and his oldest brother.

The lottery was conducted—as were the square dances, the teenage club, the Halloween program—by Mr. Summers, who had time and energy to devote to civic activities. He was a round-faced, jovial man and he ran the coal business, and people were sorry for him, because he had no children and his wife was a scold. When he arrived in the square, carrying the black wooden box, there was a murmur of conversation among the villagers, and he waved and called, "Little late today, folks." The postmaster, Mr. Graves, followed him, carrying a three-legged stool, and the stool was put in the center of the square and Mr. Summers set the black box down on it. The villagers kept their distance, leaving a space between themselves and the stool, and when Mr. Summers said, "Some of you fellows want to give me a hand?" there was a hesitation before two men, Mr. Martin and his oldest son, Baxter, came forward to hold the box steady on the stool while Mr. Summers stirred up the papers inside it.

The original paraphernalia for the lottery had been lost long ago, and the black box now resting on the stool had been put into use even before Old Man Warner, the oldest man in town, was born. Mr. Summers spoke frequently to the villagers about making a new box, but no one liked to upset even as much tradition as was represented by the black box. There was a story that the present box had been made with some pieces of the box that had preceded it, the one that had been constructed when the first people settled down to make a village here. Every year, after the lottery, Mr. Summers began talking again about a new box, but every year the subject was allowed to fade off without anything's being done. The black box grew shabbier each year; by now it was no longer completely black but splintered badly along one side to show the original wood color, and in some places faded or stained.

Mr. Martin and his oldest son, Baxter, held the black box securely on the stool until Mr. Summers had stirred the papers thoroughly with his hand. Because so much of the ritual had been forgotten or discarded, Mr. Summers had been successful in having slips of paper substituted for the chips of wood that had been used for generations. Chips of wood, Mr. Summers had argued, had been all very well when the village was tiny, but now that the population was more than three hundred and likely to keep on growing, it was necessary to use something that would fit more easily into the black box. The night before the lottery, Mr. Summers and Mr. Graves made up the slips of paper and put them in the box, and it was then taken to the safe of Mr. Summers' coal company and locked up until Mr. Summers was ready to take it to the square next morning. The rest of the year, the box was put away, sometimes one place, sometimes another;

it had spent one year in Mr. Graves' barn and another year underfoot in the post office, and sometimes it was set on a shelf in the Martin grocery and left there.

There was a great deal of fussing to be done before Mr. Summers declared the lottery open. There were the lists to make up—of heads of families, heads of households in each family, members of each household in each family. There was the proper swearing-in of Mr. Summers by the postmaster, as the official of the lottery; at one time, some people remembered, there had been a recital of some sort, performed by the official of the lottery, a perfunctory, tuneless chant that had been rattled off duly each year; some people believed that the official of the lottery used to stand just so when he said or sang it, others believed that he was supposed to walk among the people, but years and years ago this part of the ritual had been allowed to lapse. There had been, also, a ritual salute, which the official of the lottery had had to use in addressing each person who came up to draw from the box, but this also had changed with time, until now it was felt necessary only for the official to speak to each person approaching. Mr. Summers was very good at all this; in his clean white shirt and blue jeans, with one hand resting carelessly on the black box, he seemed very proper and important as he talked interminably to Mr. Graves and the Martins.

Just as Mr. Summers finally left off talking and turned to the assembled villagers, Mrs. Hutchinson came hurriedly along the path to the square, her sweater thrown over her shoulders, and slid into place in the back of the crowd. "Clean forgot what day it was," she said to Mrs. Delacroix, who stood next to her, and they both laughed softly. "Thought my old man was out back stacking wood," Mrs. Hutchinson went on, "and then I looked out the window and the kids was gone, and then I remembered it was the twenty-seventh and came a-running." She dried her hands on her apron, and Mrs. Delacroix said, "You're in time, though. They're still talking away up there."

Mrs. Hutchinson craned her neck to see through the crowd and found her husband and children standing near the front. She tapped Mrs. Delacroix on the arm as a farewell and began to make her way through the crowd. The people separated good-humoredly to let her through; two or three people said, in voices just loud enough to be heard across the crowd, "Here comes your Missus, Hutchinson," and "Bill, she made it after all." Mrs. Hutchinson reached her husband, and Mr. Summers, who had been waiting, said cheerfully, "Thought we were going to have to get on without you, Tessie." Mrs. Hutchinson said, grinning, "Wouldn't have me leave m'dishes in the sink, now, would you, Joe?" and soft laughter ran through the crowd as the people stirred back into position after Mrs. Hutchinson's arrival.

"Well, now," Mr. Summers said soberly, "guess we better get started, get this over with, so's we can go back to work. Anybody ain't here?"

"Dunbar," several people said. "Dunbar, Dunbar."

Mr. Summers consulted his list. "Clyde Dunbar," he said. "That's right. He's broke his leg, hasn't he? Who's drawing for him?"

"Me, I guess," a woman said, and Mr. Summers turned to look at her. "Wife draws for her husband," Mr. Summers said. "Don't you have a grown boy to do it for you, Janey?" Although Mr. Summers and everyone else in the village knew the answer perfectly well, it was the business of the official of the lottery to ask such questions formally. Mr. Summers waited with an expression of polite interest while Mrs. Dunbar answered.

"Horace's not but sixteen yet," Mrs. Dunbar said regretfully. "Guess I gotta fill in for the old man this year."

"Right," Mr. Summers said. He made a note on the list he was holding. Then he asked, "Watson boy drawing this year?"

A tall boy in the crowd raised his hand. "Here," he said. "I'm drawing for m'mother and me." He blinked his eyes nervously and ducked his head as several voices in the crowd said things like "Good fellow, Jack," and "Glad to see your mother's got a man to do it."

"Well," Mr. Summers said, "guess that's everyone. Old Man Warner make it?"

"Here," a voice said, and Mr. Summers nodded.

A sudden hush fell on the crowd as Mr. Summers cleared his throat and looked at the list. "All ready?" he called. "Now, I'll read the names—heads of families first—and the men come up and take a paper out of the box. Keep the paper folded in your hand without looking at it until everyone has had a turn. Everything clear?"

The people had done it so many times that they only half listened to the directions; most of them were quiet, wetting their lips, not looking around. Then Mr. Summers raised one hand high and said, "Adams." A man disengaged himself from the crowd and came forward. "Hi, Steve," Mr. Summers said, and Mr. Adams said, "Hi, Joe." They grinned at one another humorlessly and nervously. Then Mr. Adams reached into the black box and took out a folded paper. He held it firmly by one corner as he turned and went hastily back to his place in the crowd, where he stood a little apart from his family, not looking down at his hand.

"Allen," Mr. Summers said. "Anderson. . . . Bentham."

"Seems like there's no time at all between lotteries anymore," Mrs. Delacroix said to Mrs. Graves in the back row. "Seems like we got through with the last one only last week."

"Time sure goes fast," Mrs. Graves said.

"Clark. . . . Delacroix."

"There goes my old man," Mrs. Delacroix said. She held her breath while her husband went forward.

"Dunbar," Mr. Summers said, and Mrs. Dunbar went steadily to the box while one of the women said, "Go on, Janey," and another said, "There she goes."

"We're next," Mrs. Graves said. She watched while Mr. Graves came around from the side of the box, greeted Mr. Summers gravely, and selected a slip of paper from the box. By now, all through the crowd there were men holding the small folded papers in their large hands, turning them over and over nervously. Mrs. Dunbar and her two sons stood together, Mrs. Dunbar holding the slip of paper.

"Harburt. . . . Hutchinson."

"Get up there, Bill," Mrs. Hutchinson said, and the people near her laughed.

"Jones."

"They do say," Mr. Adams said to Old Man Warner, who stood next to him, "that over in the north village they're talking of giving up the lottery."

Old Man Warner snorted. "Pack of crazy fools," he said. "Listening to the young folks, nothing's good enough for them. Next thing you know, they'll be wanting to go back to living in caves, nobody work anymore, live that way for a while. Used to be a saying about 'Lottery in June, corn be heavy soon.' First thing you know, we'd all be eating stewed chickweed and acorns. There's always been a lottery," he added petulantly. "Bad enough to see young Joe Summers up there joking with everybody."

"Some places have already quit lotteries," Mrs. Adams said.

"Nothing but trouble in *that*," Old Man Warner said stoutly. "Pack of young fools."

"Martin." And Bobby Martin watched his father go forward.

"Overdyke. . . . Percy."

"I wish they'd hurry," Mrs. Dunbar said to her older son. "I wish they'd hurry."

"They're almost through," her son said.

"You get ready to run tell Dad," Mrs. Dunbar said.

Mr. Summers called his own name and then stepped forward precisely and selected a slip from the box. Then he called, "Warner."

"Seventy-seventh year I been in the lottery," Old Man Warner said as he went through the crowd. "Seventy-seventh time."

"Watson." The tall boy came awkwardly through the crowd. Someone said, "Don't be nervous, Jack," and Mr. Summers said, "Take your time, son."

"Zanini."

After that, there was a long pause, a breathless pause, until Mr. Summers, holding his slip of paper in the air, said, "All right, fellows." For a minute, no one moved, and then all the slips of paper were opened. Suddenly, all the women began to speak at once, saying, "Who is it?" "Who's got it?" "Is it the Dunbars?" "Is it the Watsons?" Then the voices began to say, "It's Hutchinson. It's Bill," "Bill Hutchinson's got it."

"Go tell your father," Mrs. Dunbar said to her older son.

People began to look around to see the Hutchinsons. Bill Hutchinson was standing quiet, staring down at the paper in his hand. Suddenly, Tessie Hutchinson shouted to Mr. Summers. "You didn't give him time enough to take any paper he wanted. I saw you. It wasn't fair!"

"Be a good sport, Tessie," Mrs. Delacroix called, and Mrs. Graves said, "All of us took the same chance."

"Shut up, Tessie," Bill Hutchinson said.

"Well, everyone," Mr. Summers said, "that was done pretty fast, and now we've got to be hurrying a little more to get done in time." He consulted his next list. "Bill," he said, "you draw for the Hutchinson family. You got any other households in the Hutchinsons?"

"There's Don and Eva," Mrs. Hutchinson yelled. "Make *them* take their chance!"

"Daughters draw with their husbands' families, Tessie," Mr. Summers said gently. "You know that as well as anyone else."

"It wasn't fair," Tessie said.

"I guess not, Joe." Bill Hutchinson said regretfully. "My daughter draws with her husband's family, that's only fair. And I've got no other family except the kids."

"Then, as far as drawing for families is concerned, it's you," Mr. Summers said in explanation, "and as far as drawing for households is concerned, that's you, too. Right?"

"Right," Bill Hutchinson said.

"How many kids, Bill?" Mr. Summers asked formally.

"Three," Bill Hutchinson said. "There's Bill, Jr., and Nancy, and little Dave. And Tessie and me."

"All right, then," Mr. Summers said. "Harry, you got their tickets back?"

Mr. Graves nodded and held up the slips of paper. "Put them in the box, then," Mr. Summers directed. "Take Bill's and put it in."

"I think we ought to start over," Mrs. Hutchinson said, as quietly as she could. "I tell you it wasn't fair. You didn't give him time enough to choose. Everybody saw that."

Mr. Graves had selected the five slips and put them in the box, and he dropped all the papers but those onto the ground, where the breeze caught them and lifted them off.

"Listen, everybody," Mrs. Hutchinson was saying to the people around her.

"Ready, Bill?" Mr. Summers asked, and Bill Hutchinson, with one quick glance around at his wife and children, nodded.

"Remember," Mr. Summers said, "take the slips and keep them folded until each person has taken one. Harry, you help little Dave." Mr. Graves took the hand of the little boy, who came willingly with him up to the box. "Take a paper out of the box, Davy," Mr. Summers said. Davy put his hand into the box and laughed. "Take just one paper," Mr. Summers said. "Harry, you hold it for him." Mr. Graves took the child's hand and removed the folded paper from the tight fist and held it while little Dave stood next to him and looked up at him wonderingly.

"Nancy next," Mr. Summers said. Nancy was twelve, and her school friends breathed heavily as she went forward, switching her skirt, and took a slip daintily from the box. "Bill, Jr.," Mr. Summers said, and Billy, his face red and his feet overlarge, nearly knocked the box over as he got a paper out. "Tessie," Mr. Summers said. She hesitated for a minute, looking around defiantly, and then set her lips and went up to the box. She snatched a paper out and held it behind her.

"Bill," Mr. Summers said, and Bill Hutchinson reached into the box and felt around, bringing his hand out at last with the slip of paper in it.

The crowd was quiet. A girl whispered, "I hope it's not Nancy," and the sound of the whisper reached the edges of the crowd.

"It's not the way it used to be," Old Man Warner said clearly. "People ain't the way they used to be."

"All right," Mr. Summers said. "Open the papers. Harry, you open little Dave's."

Mr. Graves opened the slip of paper and there was a general sigh through the crowd as he held it up and everyone could see that it was blank. Nancy and Bill, Jr. opened theirs at the same time, and both beamed and laughed, turning around to the crowd and holding their slips of paper above their heads.

"Tessie," Mr. Summers said. There was a pause, and then Mr. Summers looked at Bill Hutchinson, and Bill unfolded his paper and showed it. It was blank.

"It's Tessie," Mr. Summers said, and his voice was hushed. "Show us her paper, Bill."

Bill Hutchinson went over to his wife and forced the slip of paper out of her hand. It had a black spot on it, the black spot Mr. Summers had made the night before with the heavy pencil in the coal company office. Bill Hutchinson held it up, and there was a stir in the crowd.

"All right, folks," Mr. Summers said. "Let's finish quickly."

Although the villagers had forgotten the ritual and lost the original black box, they still remembered to use stones. The pile of stones the boys had made earlier was ready; there were stones on the ground with the blowing scraps of paper that had come out of the box. Mrs. Delacroix selected a stone so large she had to pick it up with both hands and turned to Mrs. Dunbar. "Come on," she said. "Hurry up."

Mrs. Dunbar had small stones in both hands, and she said, gasping for breath, "I can't run at all. You'll have to go ahead and I'll catch up with you."

The children had stones already, and someone gave little Davy

Hutchinson a few pebbles.

Tessie Hutchinson was in the center of a cleared space by now, and she held her hands out desperately as the villagers moved in on her. "It isn't fair," she said. A stone hit her on the side of the head.

Old Man Warner was saying, "Come on, come on, everyone." Steve Adams was in the front of the crowd of villagers, with Mrs. Graves beside him.

"It isn't fair, it isn't right," Mrs. Hutchinson screamed, and then they were upon her.

A CLOSER LOOK

Pushing her daughter's stroller down a North Bennington, Vermont, sidewalk one day in early June 1948, Shirley Jackson thought of an idea for a story. She typed it up and sent it to her literary agent the next day, hoping that some magazine would print it. Two weeks later, "The Lottery" appeared in *The New Yorker* and changed Jackson's life and reputation as an author. Those first readers were shocked, bewildered, or simply outraged, and they sent the literary magazine an unprecedented number of opinionated letters. Due to the outcry, Jackson was forced to publicly reply to her clamoring readers the next month. "Explaining just what I had hoped the story to say is very difficult," she wrote. "I suppose, I hoped, by setting a particularly brutal ancient rite in the present and in my own village to shock the story's readers with a graphic dramatization of the pointless violence and general inhumanity in their own lives."

According to the estimation of Jackson and literary scholars such as A. R. Coulthard, the brutality of "The Lottery" can be interpreted broadly as a reflection of the potential for evil that exists in every person. It is the people themselves who perpetuate the ritual. When it comes down to it, "friends"—and even relatives—will pick up stones against friends. It is every person for himself or herself. This is especially evident when Tessie Hutchinson, whose survival instincts kick in once her family is chosen to supply the victim, shamelessly tries to increase her own odds by turning on her married daughter and son-in-law. "'There's Don and Eva,' Mrs. Hutchinson yelled. 'Make *them* take their chance'" (16). But the black dot has determined Tessie's fate, and she is made the scapegoat, the representative of the community who will bear the brunt of the other members' pent-up aggressions and hidden cruelty.

The villagers do what they do simply because that is the way they have always done it. The process of the lottery has devolved into a mindless ritual—any real significance to the event has been lost. Nevertheless, ritual runs deep. The character of Old Man Warner is the primary spokesperson for tradition, and he cites an ancient saying that probably once had deeper meaning for the people of the village: "'Lottery in June, corn be heavy soon'" (14). It would seem, therefore, that the lottery is tied to the people's work ethic and productive way of life. Although the modern villagers do not pay attention to the roots of their morbid tradition, some have begun to question the continuation of the practice. They cite the fact that other communities have abandoned the lottery altogether, but that brings a sneer from Old Man Warner, who maintains that there's "'Nothing but trouble in *that*'" (14). And just as if no objections had ever been raised, just as though the people cannot think for themselves, the process continues.

While "The Lottery" and its symbolism can easily be applied to any area of human experience in which there are strict traditions, authority figures that people blindly follow, or instances where someone is made the scapegoat to cover the wrongs of others, many choose to read the tale with a Marxist bent. Karl Marx was a 19th-century German philosopher who viewed all of human history as being the history of class struggles—people of higher social classes always trying to dominate lower-class citizens. He also believed that this was because of capitalism, an economic and political system that encourages individuals to make more profits, often at the expense of others. Marx proposed that capitalism should be overthrown by communism, which would establish a society in which everything is publicly owned and all workers are placed on an even footing.

At the time of the story's publication, the United States was embarking on what would be a decades-long struggle against Communist forces in the world—the Cold War era. "The Lottery," despite Jackson's seemingly innocent intent, became too significant to be lightly dismissed as mere fiction by its readers in 1948. Fearful of Communist influence and not wanting to criticize their own form of government, perhaps the story's initial readers were outraged because they recognized the village's capitalist system as similar to their own: It is governed by an elite group of wealthier businessmen who enforce the traditions of the society. The black dot that "Mr. Summers had made the night before with the heavy pencil in the coal company office" (20) was a symbol to them that, even in America, injustice and cruelty existed. They may have concluded that this story negatively reinforced the idea that the higher-class men would remain in power over the lower-class workers indefinitely because that was the way it had always been. But such a verdict was unacceptable to those early readers who needed to believe in the security of capitalism; they needed to believe they were right, and they did not want to be reminded of the flaws in their system. It was their time to gather stones, not to develop a conscience.

Shirley Jackson

ABOUT THE AUTHOR

When questioned about the details of her life, the reticent Shirley Jackson said little except to claim that she had been born in 1919 in San Francisco, California. It was later discovered that she was actually born on December 14, 1916, but not much is known of her early life in California. Her family moved to Rochester, New York, in 1934, where the teenager experimented with her love of writing. She published her first story, "Janice," while at college in Syracuse, New York, in 1938 and continued to submit stories to such magazines as *Good Housekeeping*, *Harper's*, and *The New Yorker* throughout the next decade.

Around the same time that Jackson's first short story received acclaim from the literary world, she captured the attention of her future husband as well. Stanley Edgar Hyman was a fellow classmate and co-conspirator in Jackson's plan to create a new literary magazine on the Syracuse University campus. It was called *The Spectre* and published its first edition in the fall of 1939. In June 1940, Jackson and Hyman graduated and immediately got married. The couple began married life by moving to New York City, where Hyman was hired as an editorial assistant for *The New Republic*, a prominent journal of politics and culture.

In 1942, the couple's first son, Laurence, was born, and Jackson learned to simultaneously juggle the duties of being a writer, housewife, and mother. Three years later, the family moved to Vermont when Hyman accepted a professorship at Bennington College. Jackson also taught as a substitute for a time in a creative writing course at the college, but she did not want to make a career of teaching. Writing was her true passion. Between the births of their next three children, Jackson published her first novel, *The Road through the Wall* (1948), her most famous short story, "The Lottery" (1948), and her second novel, *Hangsaman* (1951). Jackson found the peaceful, rural setting of Vermont an ideal place to both raise her children and write productively. In fact, in 1954, she described her life as consisting of the "exports" of books and children. When surveyed for the book *Twentieth Century Authors*, Jackson responded succinctly, "I very much dislike writing about myself or my work, and when pressed for autobiographical material can only give a bare chronological outline which contains, naturally, no pertinent facts. . . . The children are Laurence, Joanne, Sarah, and Barry; my books include three novels, *The Road through the Wall*, *Hangsaman*, *The Bird's Nest*, and a collection of

Bennington College, Vermont

short stories, *The Lottery*. *Life among the Savages* is a disrespectful memoir of my children." However comically disrespectful Jackson may have been of her children in fiction, in real life, she considered her job to be motherhood, and she did that with zest. She always made time for her writing, though, whether it was in the evening when the children were asleep or in the morning while they were away at school. Nothing could interfere with her creative outlet.

In addition to the 44 short stories she published during the 1950s, Jackson also wrote her first nonfiction children's book about one

A New England witch trial

of her favorite subjects: witchcraft. She had been fascinated by the occult

for most of her life and had amassed a library of some 500 books on the

subject—some in languages she did not even understand. *The Witchcraft*

of Salem Village came out in 1956, offering a simple history of witchcraft

and a chronicle of the early Puritans' fear of the evil spirits they believed

were in their midst. The Puritans, who emigrated to the United States

from England in the mid-1600s, carried their deep religious convictions

and firmly-rooted superstitions with them, shaping the future of commu-

nity life in the new country. Jackson had a keen interest in the mentality and politics of such small-town New England life, and she brought it to this project, much as she had for "The Lottery" almost a decade before.

Despite struggling with anxiety attacks and deteriorating health in her later years, Jackson went on to write three more novels and many stories. In 1960, her novel *The Haunting of Hill House* was nominated for the National Book Award for fiction, and six years later, she received the Edgar Award for Best Short Story for "The Possibility of Evil," a tale about a malicious older woman who ironically tries to rid her town of evil. That award came too late, for Jackson had died in her sleep on August 8, 1965, and the story had been sent to the *Saturday Evening Post* for publication by her husband in December of that year. Thirty-one years later, a crate was found in the barn behind Jackson's house. The crate contained several unpublished stories, which were then turned into the 1996 collection *Just an Ordinary Day*. Jackson would have been pleased to know that her spirit had lived on.

Published by Creative Education

P.O. Box 227, Mankato, Minnesota 56002

Creative Education is an imprint of The Creative Company.

Design by Rita Marshall; production by Heidi Thompson

Page 22–31 text by Kate Riggs

Printed in the United States of America

Photographs by Alamy (Andre Jenny), Getty Images (Douglas Grundy/Three Lions)

Copyright © 2008 Creative Education

Illustrations © 2008 Etienne Delessert

Library of Congress Cataloging-in-Publication Data

Jackson, Shirley, 1916–1965.

The lottery / by Shirley Jackson

p. cm. – (Creative short stories)

ISBN 978-1-58341-584-9

I. Title. II. Series.

PS3519.A392L6 2008

813'.54—dc22   2007008487

First edition

2 4 6 8 9 7 5 3 1